W9-BAB-874

Sports Poems

Mary Colson

Heinemann
LIBRARY

Chicago, Illinois

Produced for Raintree by
White-Thomson Publishing
www.wtpub.co.uk
+44 (0)843 208 7460

Edited by Sonya Newland
Cover design by Tim Mayer
Designed by Ian Winton
Concept design by Alix Wood

Production by Victoria Fitzgerald
Originated by Capstone Global Library Ltd
Printed in the United States of America in
North Mankato, Minnesota

122017
010999R

**Library of Congress Cataloging-in-
Publication Data**
Experiencing Poetry : Sports Poems /
[compiled and edited by] Mary Colson.
    pages cm.—(Experiencing Poetry)
  Includes bibliographical references and
index.
  ISBN 978-1-4329-9561-4 (hb)—ISBN 978-
1-4329-9568-3 (pb) 1. Sports—Poetry. 2.
Poetry—Authorship. 3. Poetry—Explication.
  PN6110.S65E97 2014
  808.81'9355—dc23
  2013018342

19 18 17
10 9 8 7 6 5 4 3

Poems reproduced by permission of:
p. 8 Adam Horovitz, "Training Run,"
first published in *Turning* (Headland
Publications, 2011). Copyright © Adam
Horovitz. Reproduced by permission of
the author.
pp. 14–15 Vernon Scannell, extract from
"First Fight" reprinted by permission of the
Estate of Vernon Scannell.
p. 21 Yusef Komunyakaa, "Slam, Dunk,
& Hook" from *Pleasure Dome: New
and Collected Poems* © 2001 by Yusef
Komunyakaa. Reprinted by permission of
Wesleyan University Press. www.wesleyan.
edu/wespress
p. 27 Gail Mazur, "Ice" from *Zeppo's First
Wife*, copyright © 2005 by The University of
Chicago Press. All rights reserved. Reprinted
with permission.
p. 38 "Here's My Pitch" by Jackie Kay.
Copyright © 2012, Jackie Kay, used by
permission of The Wylie Agency (UK)
Limited.
p. 45 William Carlos Williams, "The crowd
at the ball game" ("Spring and All: (XXVII)")
from THE COLLECTED POEMS: VOLUME
I, 1909-1939, copyright ©1938 by New
Directions Publishing Corp. Reprinted by
permission of New Directions Publishing
Corp and Carcanet Press Limited (UK/
Commonwealth excluding Canada).

Cover photograph of marathon runners
reproduced with permission of Spirit of
America/Shutterstock.

Picture credits can be found on page 63.

CONTENTS

Experiencing Poems About Sports

When you hear the word "sport," what comes into your mind? Do you think of fierce competition, winners, losers, power, strength, and stamina? Or do you imagine good sports, bad sports, spoilsports, or even cheaters? Now think of poetry. What images does the word bring up in your mind? Do you expect it to look, sound, or even "be" a certain way?

The poems in this book cover different sports, and different attitudes and emotions toward them. The poet William Carlos Williams described poetry as a "field of action" where the emotions, movements, and experiences of life are played out. Just like different sports, you will see that each poem has a different set of rules. These govern how it looks and sounds, and what it means.

Whether or not a poem has a particular purpose or "message," all of the poems are deliberately shaped and crafted. Poets alter techniques to represent mood, movement, feelings, and intentions, just like an athlete in training. Look for these things as you explore each poem.

Sports and the Human Experience

The sports arena is a place where people have many different emotions and experiences. This applies to the fans as well as the players! Poets try to capture human experiences, whether they are great and glorious or painful and petty. In doing so, they face a great challenge. Imagine trying to describe the huge variety of movements that athletes make. What words capture the short, sharp actions of a boxer's punch or the graceful glide of an ice skater? The diagram below shows some words you might connect with sports. Can you think of any others?

Think About This
Sports and Poetry: A Historic Link

Poetry and sports have been linked for hundreds of years. Today, athletes from all over the world gather to participate in the Olympic Games once every four years. But did you know that the original Greek Games had poetry and musical competitions alongside sports ones? As late as 1948, the modern Olympics had gold medals for poetry!

Sports Moments

The poems in this collection cover all sorts of sports moments. They range from the intensity of a boxing match to the study of a sports crowd and the thoughts of a lonely runner. Each poem has its own unique **perspective** on an aspect of sports. They all explore how sports represent human experience, society, **motivation**, or success.

What's in a Title?

The title of the poems in this book reveal something about the poems before we even start reading them. Some tell us about the action ("Training Run," "Slam, Dunk, & Hook," "Archery"). Others tell us about the **context**, the people involved ("The crowd at the ball game"), or where the sport takes place ("Ice").

Beyond the titles, however, all sorts of different ideas arise in these poems. An idea or a meaning suggested by a word is called a **connotation**. It is helpful to think about the connotations of the title before you read a poem. For example, "Training Run" suggests a test run—a practice. "Here's My Pitch" sounds like either a sports field or someone trying to sell or promote something. "First Fight" suggests a new experience or unexplored territory. Look back at the contents page and think about the poem titles. What other connotations do they have?

MAKE A "PACT" WITH THE POEM

Most poems have a purpose and meaning. Poets choose their words carefully for deliberate effect. By reading, rereading, and thinking about the words used, you can pick out a lot of details and information. One of the first ways of accessing a poem is to make a PACT with it. Think about these points as you read a poem:

P = purpose
A = audience
C = context
T = theme

Reading for Meaning

It is always possible to understand *something* about a poem. This might be the main idea or **theme** running through it, or a sense of where it is set. Reading a poem to get a general feel for it first is an important step in experiencing poetry. Afterward, you can reread the poem and try to pick out more details.

As you read the poems in this book, ask yourself the following questions. If you can answer some of them, you are on your way to understanding the poem's content and the poet's message!

- Who is narrating the poem?
- Whose point of view is it?
- What emotions are present?
- What is the theme?
- What is the **structure**?
- What is the poet trying to achieve?
- What does the poet want the reader to feel or think?

Just as athletes need the right clothing and equipment, poets need to use certain tools when writing.

"Training Run"

P oets have written about running for over 3,000 years. The ancient Greeks wrote about the messenger Pheidippides, who ran 26 miles from the Battle of Marathon to Athens. The central character in "Training Run" is preparing for something—but what? As you read this poem, think about the contrast in the landscapes that the runner passes through. Consider also the poet's use of the five senses: sight, sound, touch, smell, and taste.

"Training Run"

by Adam Horovitz
(for Ashley Loveridge)

Linear. Beyond lines. Path swallowed
by the mare's tail flick of cow parsley.
Your feet pound out the hollowed
laughter of this discarded canal. A sparse lee

in the woods jolts you awake,
out of the hammered dream of the run;
it writhes with the scent of rain, aches
under a blanket of wild garlic, sun.

You have bitten, sharp as an arrow,
into the low heat of the dusk,
the deep focus, the valley's marrow.
The world is a husk

until you run it, until you find your way
over nettle creep, cow dung, hard-trodden clay.

Who Is the Runner?

"Training Run" is a short poem, which examines the relationship between a runner and the environments that he or she passes through. But who is the runner? Is it Ashley Loveridge, to whom Horovitz dedicated the poem? Is Ashley male or female? We cannot say for sure, but what we do know is that the **narrator** of the poem is talking to someone else—"you."

Analyzing Structure

Poets choose the words they use with great care. Look at the poem again, paying attention to the four sections. Can you see which words rhyme? Has the poet chosen a particular pattern? If so, is it the same all the way through? A deliberate pattern in poetry is called a **rhyme scheme**. You may notice that in "Training Run," Horovitz has chosen a very particular structure and rhyme scheme (called a **sonnet**). This may have influenced his ideas and his choice of verbal **imagery**.

Look also at where punctuation is used. Commas and periods break up the neat flow of the words. This may reflect the irregular rhythm of the runner as he or she moves through different landscapes.

Think About This
The "Little Song"

The sonnet, or "little song," is a type of poetry that originated in Italy in the 13th century. The poet Petrarch (1304–1374) created the form and rhyme scheme that Horovitz uses in "Training Run." Traditionally, a sonnet is a love poem. How might "Training Run" be seen in this way? Think about the love of running that is presented here. Consider how the athlete seems to be at one with the rhythm of her running and absorbed in her own world.

Movement and Sound

In "Training Run," Horovitz uses a variety of language techniques to evoke the sensations of the run. Look at the phrase he uses to describe the action of running. "Your feet pound out" is an example of active, dynamic verbs that encompass the energy of the running motion. Pounding has connotations of force and power. It also has connotations of repeated actions, which makes the running sound purposeful. The word "pound" also sounds like a noise. It is an example of **onomatopoeia**—like bang, crash, and wallop. Look back at the poem and you will see the echo of "hollowed laughter" along the old canal path, caused by the runner's feet pounding along.

METAPHOR FOR LIFE

In the last three lines of the poem, Horovitz uses the **metaphor** "The world is a husk." A husk is the protective shell of a nut, which is discarded once the food has been accessed. Saying that the world is a shell "until you run it" could be a metaphor for life. The husk might refer to the protection offered by your parents until you leave their care and set out in the world on your own. Perhaps "until you find your way / over nettle creep, cow dung, hard-trodden clay" refers to a person's life. The things described may be the problems, choices, and joys that lie in their path.

Imagery of Landscape

The runner in the poem passes through different landscapes. Pounding feet echo along a canal, swallow up countryside paths, and pass through woods in a valley. The poet uses images of nature such as "cow parsley," "wild garlic," "nettle," and "cow dung" to bring up images of the natural world, as well as vivid smells and sensations. He also paints a picture of a more neglected, human-made landscape by using phrases such as "discarded canal." These **contrasting** images suggest that the runner will experience many different aspects of the environment, in terms of both sight and smell, in the course of his or her run.

Read the poem again. Does it offer a realistic or a romanticized view of life? At the end of the poem, the narrator suggests that only through the action of running can you "find your way" through the trials of life. The "hard-trodden clay" could be a reference to the human character and personality that is gradually being formed.

ADAM HOROVITZ

1971–

Born: London, England

Adam Horovitz started writing as a child. He has done many jobs to support himself while he writes his poetry—including being a sheep dipper! He published his first collection of **verse**, *Turning*, in 2011.

Did you know?
Both of Horovitz's parents were also poets—Michael and Frances Horovitz. What can you find out about them?

In 2012, Adam Horovitz was awarded a Hawthornden Fellowship—an international literary award.

Exploring Thoughts and Responses

When you are exploring poetry, it is useful to use words like "suggests," "could mean," and "maybe" to discuss and explain your ideas about a particular poem. For example, look at the third **stanza** of "Training Run" again:

You have bitten, sharp as an arrow,
into the low heat of the dusk,
the deep focus, the valley's marrow.
The world is a husk

The bite and the arrow together *could* represent experience and time, along with "dusk," which might *suggest* the time of day. The "sun" has now become "low heat," which *could* mean that life is passing by. *Maybe* the poet means that only now, after daring to "bite," can the "deep focus" really begin. Only then can the "marrow"—or most important parts of life—really be focused on.

Think About This
Contradictions

"Training Run" begins with a contradiction. The word "linear" suggests a definite path—a fixed route. This is immediately followed with "Beyond lines," suggesting a more random, less certain direction. Why do you think the poet has done this?

Perhaps he is referring to the similarities and differences in all human lives. Or do you think he wanted to project a sense of obstacles (the cow parsley, the mare) disturbing the planned route? In other words, is the runner having to navigate unexpected obstacles to negotiate his or her path?

WRITING DOWN YOUR IDEAS

Writing down your ideas about the poems you read is a good way to find out what really interests you. It is also useful to share your feelings about a poem with other people.

One way of writing about your thoughts is to choose a quotation that you really like. Write it down and then explore the words and images it contains. Why do you like that particular quotation? What does it say to you? You can then link to another quotation from the poem and explore that, too.

POINT, EVIDENCE, EXPLAIN (P.E.E.)

Point, Evidence, Explain (P.E.E.) is another good way of writing down your thoughts and opinions about a poem.

Point: The first sentence is the *point* and this introduces your paragraph: "In 'Training Run,' Adam Horovitz uses lots of natural imagery."

Evidence: Look carefully at the poem and see what *evidence* there is to support your point: "Images like cow parsley, wild garlic, nettle, and cow dung, employ the senses of sight and smell."

Explain: Finally, you need to *explain* the effects of the words in the quotation(s). This is also where you can add your own opinion: "We usually think of nettle and cow dung as things to be avoided. I think the poet has used these words to show that the runner is in a landscape that has some hazards but is not dangerous."

"First Fight"

Vernon Scannell's "First Fight" is a long poem in four parts. The reader follows the story of the boxer's training, the fight, and what happens afterward. This extract is taken from the third part of the poem, which details the fight itself. As you read, think about all the boxing terms that Scannell uses, and consider the ways he conveys what it feels like to be a boxer.

from "First Fight"

by Vernon Scannell

Bite on gumshield
Guard held high,
The crowd are silenced,
All sounds die,
Lead with the left,
Again, again;
Watch for the opening,
Feint and then
Hook to the body
But he's blocked it and
Slammed you back
With a fierce right hand.
Hang on grimly,
The fog will clear,
Sweat in your nostrils
Grease and fear.
You're hurt and staggering,
Shocked to know
That the story's altered:
He's the hero!

But the mist is clearing,
The referee snaps
A rapid warning
And he smartly taps
Your hugging elbow
And then you step back
Ready to counter
The next attack,
But the first round finishes
Without mishap.
You suck in the air
From the towel's skilled flap.
A voice speaks urgently
Close to your ear:
'Keep your left going, Boy,
Stop him getting near.
He wants to get close to you,
So jab him off hard;
When he tries to slip below,
Never mind your guard
Crack him with a solid right,
Hit him on the chin,
A couple downstairs,
And then he'll pack it in.'

Slip in the gumshield
Bite on it hard,
Keep him off with your left,
Never drop your guard.
Try a left hook,
But he crosses with a right
Smack on your jaw
And Guy Fawkes' Night
Flashes and dazzles
Inside your skull,
Your knees go bandy
And you almost fall.
Keep the left jabbing,
Move around the ring,
Don't let him catch you with
Another hook or swing.
Keep your left working,
Keep it up high,
Stab it out straight and hard,
Again – above the eye.
Sweat in the nostrils,
But nothing now of fear,
You're moving smooth and confident
In comfortable gear.
Jab with the left again,
Quickly move away;
Feint and stab another in,
See him duck and sway.

Now for the pay-off punch,
Smash it hard inside;
It thuds against his jaw, he falls,
Limbs spread wide.
And suddenly you hear the roar,
Hoarse music of the crowd,
Voicing your hot ecstasy,
Triumphant, male and proud.

WORDS YOU MAY NOT KNOW

feint: To feint means to make a movement as if you are going to do something, then surprise your opponent by doing something different.

Guy Fawkes' Night: This is the anniversary of the day on which Guy Fawkes led a plot to blow up the British Houses of Parliament in 1605. People across Britain celebrate with fireworks and bonfires on November 5.

Action and Movement

Just like in "Training Run," the first word here is a dynamic verb—"bite." It gives the reader an immediate sense of aggressive movement, full of determination. There are other examples of this type of word in the poem, including "hook" and "slammed," as well as "crack," "hit," and "smack."

The poet uses these short, sharp words to convey a sense of action and sound. Like Horovitz, Scannell wants the reader to hear the boxing match. He wants them to experience the noise of the punches as glove makes contact with body. Scannell is able to offer his readers this intense, inside-the-ring experience because he was a boxer himself.

VERNON SCANNELL

1922–2007
Born: Aylesbury, Buckinghamshire, England

Vernon Scannell was a teacher, poet, critic, and novelist. During World War II, he fought in North Africa and France. After the war he did many jobs, including becoming a boxer, to support himself while he wrote his books and poems.

Did you know? Scannell was a sparring partner for the world light heavyweight champion boxer Freddie Mills.

British boxer Freddie Mills signs a copy of Scannell's first novel, *The Fight*, in 1953. Scannell is on the right.

The Reader's Experience

The poet deliberately uses the word "you" to help the reader identify as the boxer. His purpose, therefore, must be for the reader to experience what the boxer does. We must put ourselves in the boxing ring—receiving and throwing punches. The audience is both the reader and the fictional boxing crowd watching the match. They are mostly silent until the end of the poem when they "roar." The context and theme are the boxing match.

SEMANTIC FIELDS

A **semantic field** is a group of words all on the same theme or topic. Writers use this technique to help texts hang together well, or **cohere**. In this poem, Scannell uses a semantic field of boxing terms. This creates an intense feeling that the reader is the boxer, using the language of the sport.

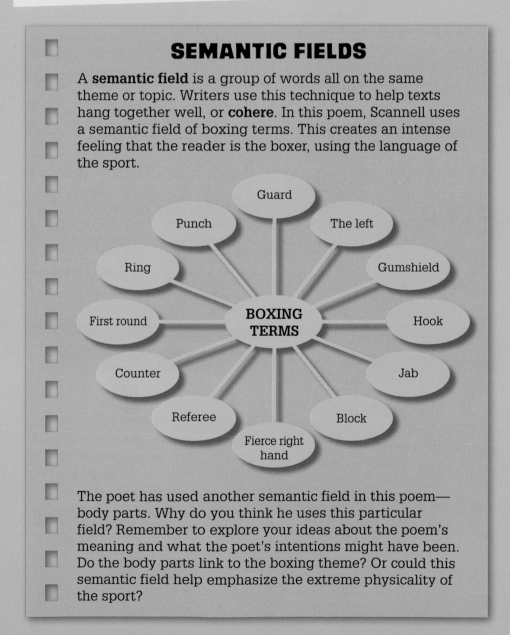

The poet has used another semantic field in this poem—body parts. Why do you think he uses this particular field? Remember to explore your ideas about the poem's meaning and what the poet's intentions might have been. Do the body parts link to the boxing theme? Or could this semantic field help emphasize the extreme physicality of the sport?

The Poem's Perspective

The story of the match is told from the perspective of a young boxer experiencing his first official fight. We hear his coach's words echoing in his mind as the boxer talks himself through the fight. Phrases like "Hang on grimly / The fog will clear" sound like the fighter is parroting another person's voice. The "fog" clears just as the first round finishes, and we hear the coach's voice as he speaks directly to the boxer. It is the same voice that we have already heard in the boxer's head.

Just as in "Training Run," the poet is telling us the story of an event in an athlete's life. Try to track the story yourself. On a piece of paper, draw a graph. Make the graph line go up and down according to when the boxer is under pressure, in trouble, and winning. What do you notice about the shape of the line?

METER

All poems have a rhythm, or **meter**. Try saying the first few lines of this extract from "First Fight" aloud. Which syllables are **stressed**, or emphasized, and which aren't? Does a pattern emerge? In this poem, the meter varies to reflect the sudden movements of the boxers. However, if you compare this to the rhythm of "Training Run," you'll notice that Horovitz uses a much more regular rhythm to convey the beat of the athlete's running strides.

The boxer Muhammad Ali wasn't just famous for his powerful punches, but also for his language. In press conferences and interviews, he often spoke in **rhyming couplets**.

Rhyme, Rhythm, and Reactions

In "First Fight," alternate lines rhyme ("Guard held high... / ...All sounds die"). The short lines, the punchy rhythm, and this alternating rhyme all help give the poem a rapid speed or **tempo**. They reflect the jagged, irregular speed of boxers dancing around the ring before throwing punches. Clipped phrases suggest fast, jerky movements as the athletes duck, dodge, and dive away from hooks and jabs.

The lines "Guy Fawkes' Night / Flashes and dazzles / Inside your skull" particularly show the power and impact of the punch the boxer receives. Think about what exploding fireworks look like, and how the poet is using this image as a metaphor for being punched really hard. The young boxer weathers the blows. He feels a metaphoric "hot ecstasy" of triumph, a wild, primitive response to throwing the knockout punch.

Think About This
A Man's Sport?

Vernon Scannell wrote this poem at a time when attitudes toward women in sports were different from attitudes today. Why do you think people once believed that boxing should be a sport just for men?

"Slam, Dunk, & Hook"

In this poem, basketball is used to explain how sports can briefly make people feel that they have been transformed into gods. The poet describes how he and his friends felt like superheroes when they played basketball in their youth. Like "Training Run," "Slam, Dunk, & Hook" has a bittersweet tone at times. However, it is also deeply **nostalgic**. It presents the past as a photograph, as though the young players are "poised in midair."

Poetry and the Past

"Slam, Dunk, & Hook" is about youthful memories, growing pains, and romanticizing the past. The reader senses that the narrator is looking back and adding or changing details about what really happened. This could be wishful thinking on the speaker's part. But it could also be nostalgia, or simply because the detail of our memories fades over time.

In the poem, an older man relates a scene from his childhood. It is an account of the joy of youth, where "we had moves we didn't know / We had." Now that the speaker is older, he can appreciate what he could not before.

MERCURY'S WINGS

The Roman god Mercury was the god of poetry and the messenger god. When Komunyakaa refers to "Mercury's / Insignia on our sneakers," he is alluding to the god's wings. The **allusion** reflects the godlike grace and speed that the youthful basketball players possessed. They felt they "could almost / Last forever," just like the god on their shoes.

"Slam, Dunk, & Hook"

by Yusef Komunyakaa

Fast breaks. Lay ups. With Mercury's
Insignia on our sneakers,
We outmaneuvered to footwork
Of bad angels. Nothing but a hot
Swish of strings like silk
Ten feet out. In the roundhouse
Labyrinth our bodies
Created, we could almost
Last forever, poised in midair
Like storybook sea monsters.
A high note hung there
A long second. Off
The rim. We'd corkscrew
Up & dunk balls that exploded
The skullcap of hope & good
Intention. Bug-eyed, lanky
All hands & feet…sprung rhythm.
We were metaphysical when girls
Cheered on the sidelines.
Tangled up in a falling.

Muscles were a bright motor
Double-flashing to the metal hoop
Nailed to our oak.
When Sonny Boy's mama died
He played nonstop all day, so hard
Our backboard splintered.
Glistening with sweat, we jibed
& rolled the ball off
Our fingertips. Trouble
Was there slapping a blackjack
Against an open palm.
Dribble, drive to the inside, feint
& glide like a sparrow-hawk.
Lay ups. Fast breaks.
We had moves we didn't know
We had. Our bodies spun
On swivels of bone & faith,
Through a lyric slipknot
Of joy, & we knew we were
Beautiful & dangerous…

WORDS YOU MAY NOT KNOW

lay ups: These are basketball shots made close to the basket and often angled in from the backboard.
labyrinth: This is a maze.
metaphysical: If something is metaphysical, is it beyond physical boundaries.

The Poetry of Memory

Many poems are about memories, trying to recapture an image or a feeling from the past. In "Slam, Dunk, & Hook," Komunyakaa looks back to a time when the world was much simpler and everything seemed possible. He recreates the physicality and energy of youth through his use of metaphors. These include "a hot / Swish of strings" to evoke the speed of the players' shoes around the basketball court.

Remember that Scannell used a semantic field of boxing terms in "First Fight." Here, Komunyakaa uses a semantic field of basketball terms to help the theme of the poem come together.

Breaks · Rim · Dunk · Lay ups · Balls · **BASKETBALL TERMS** · Drive · Sidelines · Dribble · Backboard · Metal hoop

Komunyakaa uses plenty of dynamic verbs in the poem to evoke the pace and skill of the players: "corkscrew," "dribble," "drive," and "spun."

YUSEF KOMUNYAKAA

1947–

Born: Bogalusa, Louisiana, USA

Yusef Komunyakaa enlisted in the U.S. Army after he had finished school, and he fought in the Vietnam War. His experiences there influenced some of his later poetry, but his poems cover many subjects, including issues that affect African Americans.

Did you know? In 1994, Yusef Komunyakaa was awarded the **Pulitzer Prize** for his poetry.

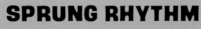

Komunyakaa once said that he thought poetry was "a way of expanding and talking around an idea or question."

SPRUNG RHYTHM

Notice how the rhythm of the basketball match is different from the rhythm of the blows traded by the boxers in "First Fight." The boxers jab, hook, and punch, while the basketball players slam and dunk. However, the players also "glide like a sparrow hawk" and "had moves we didn't know / We had." Such lines break up the neat, **staccato** rhythm of the opening lines.

Read "Slam, Dunk, & Hook" out loud. Can you hear the rhythm changing with the different sentence lengths and punctuation? This is known as **sprung rhythm**—and in fact it is the rhythm of natural speech. The poem does not allow the reader to settle into a regular beat. Instead, the poet deliberately breaks the momentum by inserting a longer line, or a pause, or a period halfway through a line. Komunyakaa even describes the movement of the players as "All hands & feet...sprung rhythm." This reflects their youthful athleticism as well as their slight awkwardness.

Exploring Meaning

The metaphoric nature of "Slam, Dunk, & Hook" is a key element of the poem. Komunyakaa goes beyond the basketball game to evoke the glories of youth. It is through this central metaphor that the players' life experiences, or **rites of passage**, are described. There is a reference to showing off in front of the cheering girls on the sidelines. At this point, the players become "metaphysical," or otherworldly. Their "Muscles were a bright motor / Double-flashing." These lines evoke a sense of power and effortlessness.

The death of a parent is linked to the game. The poet also uses a device known as **personification**, where nonhuman objects or concepts are given human characteristics. The personification in this poem is "Trouble," which is waiting for everyone at some point in their lives. The players' talent contrasts with these sometimes harsh realities, as they "glide like a sparrow-hawk," forgetting the real world for a short while.

The **juxtaposition** in the closing lines ("we knew we were / Beautiful & dangerous") introduces a bittersweet note. The players have created a sporting image of great beauty on the court, but what does the word "dangerous" refer to? Could it mean the "Trouble" waiting off the court? Perhaps it links to the players' sense of invincibility. Are the young men "dangerous" because they are so sure of themselves? Does their confidence blind them to the dangers ahead?

Think About This
How Reliable Are Memories?

What do you think Komunyakaa is saying in this poem about the reliability of memory? Do you think he is recalling his youth exactly as it happened? We often look back on past events and think differently from how we felt at the time. For some people, this is a way of blurring painful memories. Sometimes we even romanticize our past or our achievements. Do you think there is anything wrong with this? How do our memories sometimes deceive us and make us unreliable narrators? Is there an event that you recall differently from someone else? Can you both be right? Does it matter?

Abstract Ideas

In the last few lines of "Slam, Dunk, & Hook," the poet uses four **abstract** words: two nouns (faith and joy) and two adjectives (beautiful and dangerous). Abstract words refer to things you cannot touch or hold. All four of these words will mean something slightly different to everyone. Komunyakaa associates these words with his youth. "Faith," "joy," and "beautiful" are idealistic words that create a sense of perfection, while "dangerous" hints at an unknown menace or threat to this memory of childhood. This suggests that the older man knows that what followed was not all perfect.

"Ice"

Like "Slam, Dunk, & Hook," this poem is about memories. In "Ice," the poet concentrates on the memory of a quieter and less public occasion—that of a "shy girl" skating with her father.

What Is the Poem About?

"Ice" is not about a fast-paced activity like basketball, but a gentler, more flowing sport. It offers an adult's perspective on a child's experience of ice skating with her father. It could be the adult looking back on her own childhood, or perhaps the events described are occurring as the poet watches. The poem is written in the present tense. This makes the action much more immediate than if it were written in the past tense.

The poem's emotional force comes from the suggestion that this time the girl shares with her father will not last forever. Mazur writes that the love between father and child is "perfect." There is a bittersweet tone as she explains that no one will ever love the girl in quite the same way.

The Context of the Poem

It is not easy to work out the context of "Ice." It does not seem that the poet is writing in response to a specific event. However, the reader is given some direct references in terms of geography. Ware's Cove is a real place in Massachusetts, so the city the men come from with the wooden barriers would be Boston. As you read the poem, think about what themes are present—childhood, parents and children, regret?

LANGUAGE CONTRASTS

Read the poem opposite. Do you notice the contrasts? Look for references to hot and cold, and to noise and silence. Consider all the words that reflect the temperature: "warming," "stove," "cozy," "frozen," "ice," and "chafed." Think about how they suit the environment they describe. Now look at the sound words: "clumping," "playing," and "slamming." These contrast with the language used for the "shy girl" and her father, who skate without music. This suggests that no one else sees them—they are alone as they "glide arm in arm onto the blurred surface together."

"Ice"

by Gail Mazur

In the warming house, children lace their skates,
bending, choked, over their thick jackets.

A Franklin stove keeps the place so cozy
it's hard to imagine why anyone would leave,

clumping across the frozen beach to the river.
December's always the same at Ware's Cove,

the first sheer ice, black, then white
and deep until the city sends trucks of men

with wooden barriers to put up the boys'
hockey rink. An hour of skating after school,

of trying wobbly figure-8's, an hour
of distances moved backwards without falling,

then—twilight, the warming house steamy
with girls pulling on boots, their chafed legs

aching. Outside, the hockey players keep
playing, slamming the round black puck

until it's dark, until supper. At night,
a shy girl comes to the cove with her father.

Although there isn't music, they glide
arm in arm onto the blurred surface together,

braced like dancers. She thinks she'll never
be so happy, for who else will find her graceful,

find her perfect, skate with her
in circles outside the emptied rink forever?

Setting the Scene

The poem covers four "scenes," which describe the house, the rink before the hockey match, the match, and the rink after everyone else has gone, when the girl and her father skate. Each scene has its own distinctive language and imagery.

The house that the children get ready in is remote. We know this because the poet situates the house for her readers—it is by the "frozen beach" at "Ware's Cove." In addition, we learn that the house is heated by a wood-burning stove—something more common in the countryside. All these details may suggest that the poem is **autobiographical**.

MOTIFS

In this poem, ice is the central **motif**—the main image, theme, or symbol. Here, it clearly represents more than just the frozen beach. Mazur uses the ice motif as a way of capturing a memory. The ice preserves the moment in the poet's mind, and keeps that image of the girl and her father "frozen" forever.

People and Movement

The depiction of the rink is as **anonymous** as that of the house. The poet refers to "children," "men," "boys," "girl," and "father," but none of them is given a specific identity. They just revolve around the rink at different times. The children can skate after school, while twilight is for the hockey players. Only "at night" can the shy girl and her father come to the cove to skate.

Notice the poet's use of movement images in the poem, from the "wobbly figure-8's" of the children to the "slamming the round black puck" of the hockey players. In further contrast to these images is the "glide" of the girl and her father. The **simile** "braced like dancers" suggests a graceful motion—a happy understanding between the two.

GAIL MAZUR

1938–

Born: USA

Gail Mazur went to Smith College, in Massachusetts, and studied poetry with the famous American poet, Robert Lowell. She published her first poetry collection at the age of 40. She is a founding director of the Blacksmith House Poetry Center in Cambridge, Massachusetts. This is a workshop, performance space, and support community for writers.

Did you know? In 2001, Gail Mazur's collection *They Can't Take That Away From Me* was shortlisted for the prestigious American National Book Award.

Gail Mazur's fifth book of poetry, *Zeppo's First Wife*, won the Massachusetts Book Award in Poetry in 2006.

Purpose and Point of View

It can be difficult to figure out why a poet wrote a particular poem. When considering the purpose of a poem and its point of view, it is useful to explore several options. Mazur might have written "Ice" as a way of remembering her own father. Or she could be writing less autobiographically and more imaginatively about scenes from childhood that we all feel are precious. The broad theme of snow, ice, and wintry weather may have been intended to appeal to a wide readership. These are things that most people can relate to.

EMOTIVE LANGUAGE

Emotive language is the use of words that generate feelings and emotions in the reader. It can be any emotion at all, from laughter to tears, from horror to shock. In "Ice," Mazur generates many feelings in the reader. These include a sense of loss and sadness, and even pity for the older voice looking back to a time that is gone.

Pathos is a particular kind of emotive language. It comes from the Greek word for "pity." In literature, pathos refers to writing that makes the reader feel this emotion. When reading "Ice," we feel a sense of pathos in response to the shy girl and the thought that "she'll never be so happy." The final metaphor of the "emptied rink" suggests that the father is no longer alive. This adds another layer of pathos to the poem.

Reflection and Poetic Voice

The poem occasionally hints that the speaker is an older voice looking back to the past. The first example of this comes in the fourth line: "it's hard to imagine why anyone would leave." Adults and children often have very different views on venturing out into the snow on cold days. The line suggests an older narrator who, looking back, cannot believe she ever wanted to leave the warmth of the house.

A second example of this older voice coming through is in the metaphor at the end: "skate with her in circles forever." This image has connotations of unconditional love and parental protection that suggest a mature speaker.

Think About This
Circles

What do you think the "circles" might represent? Are they just referring to the movements of the skaters, or could they be a metaphor for time? Think about the shape of a clock face and how circles and time are often connected. What about metaphorical protection—could the circles form protective barriers? What else might the circles suggest?

"Archery"

In the next poem, John Kendrick Bangs uses the sport of archery to make observations about relationships. He turns archery into a metaphor for human behavior. Archery is an ancient sport. The poet makes a link between this and how men and women act toward each other. Try to work out who are the archers and who are the targets.

The Poetic Voice

As you read the poem, you may notice that it has quite a different tone from the others in this book. The narrator here speaks lightheartedly, in contrast with the intensity of the speaker in "First Fight," for example, or the nostalgic tone of "Ice."

In the poem, women are presented as archers or hunters, and the men their targets or prey. The poet wants us to feel sorry for men, but he is also gently mocking them because of their weakness when confronted by a pretty face. Although the narrator is making fun of men, he seems to accept his role as the target of the female archers.

JOHN KENDRICK BANGS

1862–1922
Born: Yonkers, New York, USA

John Kendrick Bangs was a highly respected magazine journalist. He was a **satirist** and his articles poked gentle fun at New York's upper class.

Did you know? The novelist Mark Twain, author of *The Adventures of Tom Sawyer*, once joked that he was going to run for the presidency with Kendrick Bangs as his running mate.

John Kendrick Bangs once ran for Mayor of New York.

"Archery"

by John Kendrick Bangs

"Archery's come in again!"
So the Sporting Writers shout.
I should like to know just when
Archery was ever out.
Long as I have been alive
Archers bold and archers fair
Have been ruthless with the drive
Of their arrows everywhere.

There is Polly—archery
Is her best accomplishment.
Scores a bull's-eye clear and free
Every time her bow is bent.
True, an arrow seldom flies
When the lady snaps the chord—
She just merely lifts her eyes
And the hit is duly scored.

Then Myrtilla—you should see
Fair Myrtilla take a shot!
Makes her hits three out of three,
Not a miss in all the lot.
Myrtle's arrows they are smiles,
Sped to pierce the human heart—
She, like Polly, uses wiles
Substituted for the dart.

Daphne too is champion
In the arts of archery.
She's a marvel on the run
Where the best of archers be.
Not a target in the world
But doth score when Daphne shoots,
Though no arrow e'er is hurled—
Glances are her substitutes.

'Ware these archer maids, O man!
They are too expert for you.
Watch and ward you if you can,
For their aim is deadly true.
You may think yourself the "beau"
In this little shooting game,
But you'll find before you know
You're the target just the same!

Structure of the Poem

The poem is divided into five stanzas. The first and last stanzas act as introduction and conclusion, and the middle three give examples of different women and how they are acting flirtatiously. Each stanza has eight lines, grouped into two rhyming sections of four lines each. The rhyme scheme is ABABCDCD—alternate lines rhyme. This helps give the poem a lighthearted tone.

POETIC TONE

Tone refers to the mood or atmosphere generated by the voice in a poem. If you look back through the poems in this book so far, you will see that each one is written in a different tone. Some are more serious, sad, or thoughtful than others. In "Archery," the poetic tone is one of amusement. The rhyme scheme contributes to the humorous tone of the poem. The use of exaggeration—in the form of exclamation marks —also suggests that the speaker does not really mind the women playing games.

The Greek god of love, Eros, and his Roman equivalent, Cupid, are often represented holding bows and arrows.

Theme and Purpose

The reader is given an insight into the poet's purpose and theme in the first stanza. Here, the narrator makes it clear what his theme will be:

> Archers bold and archers fair
> Have been ruthless with the drive
> Of their arrows everywhere.

In other words, women are the archers and they mercilessly target men with their "arrows"—their looks, flirtations, and cunning, or **guile**. The metaphor "the arts of archery" is extended throughout the poem as the women's smiles and eyes "pierce the human heart" of men.

Presentation of Women

The three women in the middle stanzas are Polly, Myrtilla, and Daphne. They represent the poet's idea of "typical" female identities. They have characteristics of ancient goddesses. Think of the two ways the letters b-o-w can be pronounced. Polly "snaps the chord" of the bow (weapon) and "lifts her eyes" from her bow (curtsy). Myrtilla's "arrows" are her "smiles" and "**wiles**." Daphne, who is named after a beautiful woman/spirit in ancient Greek **mythology**, only has to "glance" to hit the target. The poet, therefore, presents women as insincere, cunning, and manipulative. But is he critical of women? Or is he secretly impressed by their skill?

Think About This
Love, Poetry, and Archery

Since the earliest times, archery and poetry have been interlinked. Apollo was the Greek god of the Sun, truth, music, poetry, and archery. Poets have often used archery and the target as a metaphor to represent love and relationships. Even today, we use metaphors to do with hearts and arrows to suggest being in love, like being struck by Cupid's arrow. Can you think of other sports metaphors, such as the "thrill of the chase" or "to play ball"?

Language of Comparison

In the first stanza, the "arrows everywhere" implies that there is no escape—that men are powerless to resist the superior "archer maids... / They are too expert for you." Elsewhere, words such as "flies," "sped," and "shoots" have connotations of speed. They relate to the flashing looks and smiles between men and women, hinting at the instant effect they have. The "shooting game" that the poet refers to in the final stanza is a summary of previous language, including "the hit," "the shot," and "the dart." The "game" is **ironic**, as the consequences are serious for the injured men.

Think About This
A PACT with "Archery"

What do you think is the PACT of this poem? Consider why the poet might have chosen to write such a piece. Also think about who the audience might be—the "you" that the poet is addressing.

Read the last stanza again. Is Kendrick Bangs writing a **cautionary tale** to warn young men of the tricks women play while dating? What do you think "Watch and ward" means? Finding out when the poem was written and then reflecting on its themes should allow you to suggest some possibilities for the poem's PACT.

COMPARING AND CONTRASTING POEMS

Comparing poems can help us see connections between them and make the ideas in each stand out. For example, you could compare and contrast the theme of love as presented in "Archery" and "Slam, Dunk, & Hook." You could say that the two poems are both about childhood memories but are written from different points of view, with different tones. One of the ways you might compare the poems is to look at the poetic techniques they use, or the attitudes the poets have toward the theme.

MAD COW, FAT HEN
Whatever poems you are comparing, and whatever your focus for comparison, you need a vocabulary to express this. MAD COW and FAT HEN are a good way of remembering many different comparison words. They are also a good way of remembering words to express your developing ideas.

M = meanwhile	F = furthermore
A = additionally	A = although
D = during	T = therefore
C = consequently	H = however
O = otherwise	E = even though
W = whereas	N = nevertheless

These words can be used to signal the change from writing about one poem to writing about another, as well as for developing ideas. For example:

John Kendrick Bangs focuses on the humor of the vulnerable men who are the target of pretty women, <u>whereas</u> Yusef Komunyakaa concentrates on the love of the game and the power, energy, and sense of immortality the basketball players feel.

Try using the MAD COW FAT HEN words when you write about and discuss poems.

"Here's My Pitch"

Jackie Kay wrote this poem for Sheffield United, a soccer club in the United Kingdom, as part of the Kick It Out! campaign to rid English soccer of racism. She delivered her poem before a game, addressing the whole stadium of players, officials, and fans. As you read the poem, think about how Jackie Kay uses soccer terms to deliver her anti-racism message.

"Here's My Pitch"

by Jackie Kay

Let Arthur Wharton come back from the dead
To see the man in black blow the final whistle.
Let the game of two halves be beautiful,
Not years ahead. Let every kissing of the badge,
Every cultured pass, every lad and lass,
Every uttered thought, every chant and rant,
Every strip and stripe – be free of it.

Then football would have truly played a blinder,
And Arthur returned to something kinder.
Let the man in black call time on racism.
And Arthur will sing out on the wings,
Our presiding spirit – the first black blade.
Imagine having everything to play for.
This is our pitch. Now hear us roar.

WHARTON AND SHEFFIELD UNITED

Arthur Wharton was the first black soccer player in the English soccer league. He was born in Ghana, Africa, to a half-Scottish, half-Grenadian father and a Ghanaian mother. He went to England in 1882 and played for Sheffield United. Also, Sheffield United players are called "The Blades" because of the city's reputation for steel production.

Sports and Society

At the time Kay wrote "Here's My Pitch," there had been several racist incidents at soccer games, involving fans as well as players. The poet's attitude toward racism is very clear as she says "Let the man in black call time on racism." The man in black is the referee and to "call time" means to put a stop to something, just like the referee blows the whistle to signal the end of the game. Kay was inspired by Wharton's story. In the poem, she imagines him coming back from the dead to hear the news of the racist incidents in the game.

There are a lot of references in the poem to the loyalty and passion of both the players and the fans. When soccer players score a goal, they often kiss their team's badge on their shirts. This show of loyalty is welcomed by many of the fans who "chant and rant" on the terraces. "Rant" also has connotations of loud, angry, uncontrolled argument. Kay uses it to show the ugly side of language used in the stands.

Think About This
Racism in Sports

Think about your favorite sport. Does it suffer from racism? Remember that racism isn't just about color, but about treating people from other countries differently, too. Unfortunately, racism is still common in sports and can involve fans as well as players. Are there anti-racism campaigns in your sport already? What kinds of activities or campaigns do you think would help improve things and really make a difference?

Reading for Meaning

Jackie Kay begins her poem with a simple wish: "Let." This is the first of several words in the poem that are like prayers and blessings. She repeats the word in the opening stanza. Both times she goes on to make a request for something to happen. She wants a return to a time where there was a sense of racial acceptance and dignified play between competing teams. In the first verse, the word "racism" is never actually used; that only comes in the second stanza, when the purpose of the poem is made clear.

PLAYING WITH POETIC STRUCTURE

Kay uses the sonnet form to express both her love of the game and her hatred of racism. Sonnets have 14 lines and end with a rhyming couplet. Kay does not follow the traditional rhyme scheme of a sonnet, but she does finish her poem with a couplet. Compare how this structure is different from that used in "Training Run." Why might the poets have taken different approaches to the sonnet form? Think about the different themes and attitudes expressed in the poems.

Soccer is known as the "beautiful game" in reference to its graceful simplicity when played well.

Jackie Kay adopts overused phrases, or **clichés**, to express her real message, that of a call for an end to racism in soccer. The "game of two halves" is the match itself. Of course, a soccer game has two halves. But the phrase also refers to when one team is on top in one half and then the other team plays better in the second half.

Think About This
The Roaring Crowd

Jackie Kay is requesting "calling time" on racism, just like the referee will call time to signal the end of a match. The onomatopoeic "roar" at the end of the poem suggests an impatient crowd shouting for both the game and racial justice. "Roar" suggests a wild noise or untamed anger. Think about the context the poem was delivered in. Jackie Kay was in a soccer stadium prior to kickoff. How does the "roar" work in two ways? How does it show the crowd's approval for her request?

JACKIE KAY

1961–
Born: Edinburgh, Scotland

Jackie Kay is an acclaimed poet, playwright, and fiction writer. Her writing explores issues of identity, voice, and emotions. Born to a Scottish mother and Nigerian father, Jackie Kay was adopted by a white couple at birth. She explored her search for a cultural identity and the experience of growing up within a white family in her award-winning poetry collection *The Adoption Papers*.

Did you know? Kay has won various prizes for her writing, including the Somerset Maugham Award.

Kay wrote a book about her search for her biological parents, called *Red Dust Road*, in 2010.

Internal Rhyme and Sound Effects

Traditionally, poetry is meant to be read aloud and heard. So, sound effects such as rhyme, **alliteration**, and hard letter sounds like k, d, c, t, and ch are all part of a poet's toolkit. Kay wrote this poem to be performed before the crowd and players at a real soccer game, so she would have chosen and arranged her words very carefully. She wanted her central message not just to be clear to everyone, but also to be hard-hitting and memorable. Read "Here's My Pitch" aloud and try to identify the sound effects. Consider how these contribute to the emotion of the poem.

EXAMPLES OF INTERNAL RHYME

A great deal of poetry, including "Archery," uses **end rhymes**—where only the last words in the lines rhyme. Kay uses some end rhymes like a traditional sonnet does, but she also breaks the end-rhyme pattern with **internal rhymes**. This is where a word in the middle of a line rhymes with other words in the poem.

As an example, look at the end of the first line in "Here's My Pitch." The word "dead" has a corresponding rhyme with "ahead" in the fourth line. Now look at "badge" at the end of line 4. This word is part-rhymed with "pass," "lad," "lass," "chant," and "rant." Rhyme lists like this emphasize the poet's message—the single-syllable words are punched out as a way of underlining the theme.

Analyzing Title and Theme

The title of the poem "Here's My Pitch" indicates that this is the poet's list of suggestions for a racism-free game. The double meaning of the word "pitch" plays with the actual soccer field as well as meaning a presentation of ideas or views. The use of the **pronoun** "my" suggests something personal and even original. The title also has the feel of a declaration with its strong sense of ownership, "my pitch." It's as if the spectators need to ready themselves to pay attention. The poet cleverly plays with the title in the last line of the poem, when she changes the pronouns from "my" to "our" and "us." This way, she includes the audience and shares the ownership of the idea.

SPORTS RITUALS

Most sports have a tradition of honoring the players before the competition begins. National anthems may be played, hands might be shaken, respectful bows are sometimes exchanged, and even war dances are sometimes performed. What do you think would be the best way of honoring the opposition?

"The crowd at the ball game"

"The crowd at the ball game" is a challenging poem, and you may need to read it several times to make sense of it. It focuses on the people watching the baseball game rather than those playing it. The poet watches the crowd closely and records their delight, beauty, and ugliness as they react to events on the field. As you read, try to work out what the poet's attitude toward the crowd is.

The Crowd's Emotions

The poem begins by acknowledging that despite the cheers and wishes of the crowd, they are essentially powerless to change the outcome of the game, because they are not actually participating. Williams hints that the crowd feels a sense of relief that they are not responsible for the success or failure of their team.

Despite this, the spectators draw excitement from the "chase / and the escape, the error / the flash of genius." The dramatic language suggests a piece of theater. But beneath the surface a less pleasing sensation exists, in total contrast to the "beauty" that is stated overtly by the poet.

WILLIAM CARLOS WILLIAMS

1883–1963
Born: Rutherford, New Jersey, USA

William Carlos Williams wrote short stories, plays, novels, essays, and an autobiography, as well as poetry. He was friends with the poet Ezra Pound, who was a great influence on Williams's early work.

Did you know? Williams was a professional doctor and pediatrician who managed to carry on his literary career alongside his medical one.

Williams belonged to an artistic movement known as "Imagism," which believed in using simple words in free verse.

"The crowd at the ball game"

by William Carlos Williams

The crowd at the ball game
is moved uniformly

by a spirit of uselessness
which delights them—

all the exciting detail
of the chase

and the escape, the error
the flash of genius—

all to no end save beauty
the eternal—

So in detail they, the crowd,
are beautiful

for this
to be warned against

saluted and defied—
It is alive, venomous

it smiles grimly
its words cut—

The flashy female with her
mother, gets it—

The Jew gets it straight—it
is deadly, terrifying—

It is the Inquisition, the
Revolution

It is beauty itself
that lives

day by day in them
idly—

This is
the power of their faces

It is summer, it is the solstice
the crowd is

cheering, the crowd is laughing
in detail

permanently, seriously
without thought

Reading Between the Lines

Poets often refer to ideas or subjects beyond the poem itself. This is a way of alluding to connected themes or contexts. In this poem, Williams alludes to many things about the crowd and its prejudices. Suggesting something rather than directly explaining or telling something is called **inference**. This can be exciting to explore in poetry.

The Two Faces of the Crowd

The poet is clearly transfixed by the crowd rather than the baseball game. He thinks the spectators are getting carried away, and that perhaps they have forgotten that it is just a game. He believes that outcome does not really matter—the players play "to no end." Life will go on as it did before, no matter who wins the game.

Like Jackie Kay, Williams seems to infer that the crowd is racist. The line "The Jew gets it straight" could mean that a Jewish player on the field is insulted. It might also mean that a Jewish person understands the hatred the crowd has for the other team. The ugliness of this sentiment contrasts with the "beauty" the poet also sees in the crowd. Without the crowd there, the game isn't "beautiful"—it is just players in an empty stadium.

Williams feels that the crowd can add a positive atmosphere and play their part in an exciting and beautiful piece of entertainment.

Negativity in the Poem

The stadium is gripping, but there is a threatening and sinister undertone to Williams's line "venomous it smiles grimly." Here, it is as if the poet is unnerved or even frightened by the poisonous feelings the crowd shows and the ugly consequences of racism and hatred.

The poem ends on a somewhat despairing note. Williams suggests the crowd acts "without thought" like Roman Catholic Inquisitors and French Revolutionaries. These are examples of historical groups who terrorized, tortured, and killed people they saw as their enemies. The serious underlying suggestion is that history is repeating itself. The poet is concerned that humans have not progressed beyond tribal instincts, which abuse others as a way of exerting power. The threat is always there, lying just below the surface of human nature. This is because it "lives day by day in them idly," waiting for another occasion to emerge.

Think About This
Bad Behavior

Sports fans have always been loud and passionate. In ancient Rome, the crowd bayed for blood as gladiators fought to the death. Even today, fans "live" the game with their heroes and cheer on their teams until they are hoarse. Have you ever been to a sports event where you acted differently because you were part of a crowd? Why do you think that was? Were you surprised at your own behavior?

The Romans loved sports—the more bloodthirsty the better!

Pace of the Poem

Williams uses many poetic techniques to quicken, slow, and pause the speed at which "The crowd at the ball game" is read. There are no periods in the poem, so the reader has to decide where to pause. This can affect how the images are created in the reader's mind, and reflects the varying pace of the baseball game being watched.

ENJAMBMENT

A lot of modern poetry doesn't have periods at the end of each line. "The crowd at the ball game" is like this. Read the poem aloud. How do you have to read it for the phrases to make sense? You cannot stop at the end of each line. Instead, you have to run on over the end of a line and onto the next one for the meaning to be clear.

This technique is called **enjambment**. Enjambment is a way of breaking up the rhythm of a poem. It controls the pace of the poem, not letting the reader go on too quickly. Enjambment can also be a way of emphasizing key words at the beginning of a new line. Look back at the other poems in the book to see how enjambment slows or quickens the pace, and how it affects the delivery of a poem. Note also how Williams includes a lot of dashes, which have a similar, stop-start effect.

Comparing Poems: FLIRT

When you compare and contrast poems, it is helpful to organize your thoughts and to FLIRT a little! Form, Language, Imagery, Response, and Techniques (FLIRT) are the key areas to cover.

Think about "The crowd at the ball game" and "Here's My Pitch." These are both poems about people's reactions to both sports and the players, but they go beyond that too. Williams's poem is about how people can change during the course of watching a baseball game. Kay's poem is about encouraging people in the crowd to act differently, in a non-racist way.

Taking extracts from the poems and exploring ideas about them will help you shape and order your thoughts. Remember that creating a FLIRT table is just a starting point. There are many more points of comparison that could be added to make your response more personal and individual.

	"The crowd at the ball game"	"Here's My Pitch"
Form	Natural speech, enjambment	Sonnet, enjambment
Language	Criticism and reactions of the crowd	Requests an end to racism in soccer, prayer-like, semantic field of soccer
Imagery	The crowd as a creature	The soccer field, the referee, the players
Response	What is your response to the poem? Why did William Carlos Williams write the poem?	What is your response and is it the one the poet expected or engineered you to have? Why did Jackie Kay write the poem?
Techniques	Metaphor, abstract ideas, bittersweet tone at end	Metaphor, cliché, listing

What Have We Learned?

"**S**port" can mean many things and has many different connotations, from good sport and spoilsport, to amateur games and competitive sports. There is also a fine line between sporting success and failure, fulfillment and disappointment. Sports poetry, therefore, can take many different forms and attitudes.

Every poem is unique, so it is important to approach each new poem you read with an open mind. Poets are not out to trick you. They use different language and style techniques to make a poem effective and memorable. Poetic techniques, themes, and structure are just part of the toolkit at a poet's disposal. Depending on the purpose, audience, and context, the poet will decide which "tools" to use. Remember to begin with whatever facts or details you know and work from there.

The chart opposite shows you one way to begin exploring a new poem.

Back to the Start

Look back at the poems in this book and remind yourself what your first thoughts and feelings about them were. Then think about all that you have read, learned, and considered about them.

The approaches suggested in this book should give you the confidence to explore more poetry.

Exploring Poetry

The best approach to a poem is to explore different possibilities or interpretations. To begin with, concentrate on the lines and images you understand and work with those. Later, when you have looked at the poem a few more times, other things will start to emerge. It is very rare to understand a poem on the first reading. Reading a poem is not the same as reading a novel—poets *want* you to read their work a few times.

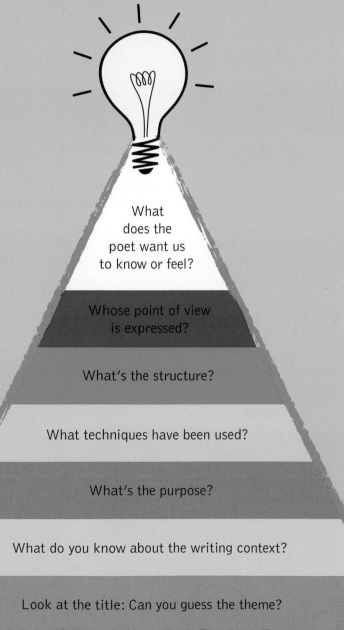

What does the poet want us to know or feel?

Whose point of view is expressed?

What's the structure?

What techniques have been used?

What's the purpose?

What do you know about the writing context?

Look at the title: Can you guess the theme?

Exploring More

What was your favorite poem in this book? What was so special about it? Did you like its clever use of techniques or did you admire the way the attitudes and opinions were expressed?

If You Liked...

"Training Run" by Adam Horovitz: You might like "The Song of the Ungirt Runners" by Charles Hamilton Sorley. Sorley wrote it during his training as an army officer during World War I. He was killed a few weeks later, at the age of just 20.

"First Fight" by Vernon Scannell: Try reading the whole poem. Follow the young boxer through his dreams and his training to the fight and beyond. You could also look up the poem "The Ballad of Billy Rose" by Leslie Norris—a bittersweet poem about a blind boxer.

"Slam, Dunk, & Hook" by Yusef Komunyakaa: You could explore other poems about basketball, such as "Old Men Playing Basketball" by B. H. Fairchild.

"Ice" by Gail Mazur: Try "Kata" by Lavinia Greenlaw. This abstract poem can be interpreted in many different ways.

"Archery" by John Kendrick Bangs: Try reading "The Ballad of Agincourt" by Michael Drayton, which describes the skill of the archers during a war.

There is a sports poem for every single activity, contest, and emotion.

"Here's My Pitch" by Jackie Kay: Check out what your favorite sports or local club is doing to stop racism. You could also read about Jesse Owens, the African American athlete who competed at the 1936 Olympic Games in Berlin, Germany, with Hitler looking on.

"The crowd at the ball game" by William Carlos Williams: "Lines Composed on the Occasion of Manchester United's Champions League Defeat by Bayern Munich in April 2010" by Michael Symmons Roberts might interest you. Here, the fan is metaphorically on the field with his team, living and breathing every move.

Think About This
Following Up

Remember, exploring a theme you enjoy or a structure can lead you off in all sorts of exciting directions. Look at the diagram below. These are the different aspects of sports you've already explored in this book. Which one are you going to check out next?

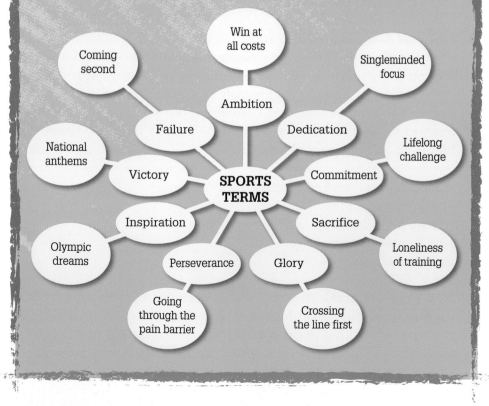

Write Your Own Sports Poem

Writing poetry is an exciting challenge. Playing with style and words until you get down exactly what you want to say is a satisfying way of expressing yourself. Remember that you can write about sports from many different perspectives—that of the players, the coaches, the crowds...

Here are 10 easy steps that can help you write your own sports poem.

1. Find a quiet space free from distractions. Gather together paper and pens and set up your writer's desk. (TIP: It is good to sit near a window, where you can look out and get inspiration.)

2. Choose one aspect of sports from the diagram on page 53. Think carefully about your choice. The more you can identify with your chosen theme, the better. For example, you might be an athlete crossing the line first (or last); an older person looking at young athletes playing a sport; or nervously waiting for the starting gun to go off.

3. Consider how you are going to represent that aspect of sports. For example, if you are going to write about victory, what moment are you going to focus on? Crossing the line or getting the medal? Are you going to use the gold medals as a metaphor? (TIP: Note down all your ideas. Don't cross anything out at this stage. The more ideas you have to choose from, the better.) Try using these ideas and starting lines to help you:

    A basketball court with rain beating on the tarmac...
    The net bulging as the ball hits it...
    A tennis player bouncing a ball on hot, red clay...
    I am the road you run along...
    I am the court you...

4. Now think about the structure you want to use. Do you want to go for **free verse** with enjambment, or are you going to set yourself the challenge of sticking to the sonnet form like Jackie Kay and Adam Horowitz? (TIP: If you are going to write a sonnet, it's a good idea to map out the lines and rhyme scheme before you begin.)

5. What techniques will be most effective and relevant to use? If you are going to write about training and using gym equipment or machines then onomatopoeia, personification, similes, and metaphors might best create the sound and description. If you are writing about something more personal like playing a sport with a special person or in a special place you might want to use some of the abstract ideas that Yusef Komunyakaa and Gail Mazur used. Of course, if you are going to write about how hopeless you are at sport, you'll probably use some humor!

6. What is your title going to be? Is it going to be emotive like "Ice," symbolic like "Here's My Pitch," or straightforward like "First Fight"?

7. What's your purpose? Is it to protest or inform, entertain or suggest?

8. Who is your audience? Is it young children, adults, or people your own age?

9. Look back at all the notes you've made so far. Which ones do you want to keep? Which ones are you going to save for another poem?

10. Take a deep breath. Feel how your body moves as you breathe. Think about your five senses and how they react. Now you're ready to start writing!

Star Tips for Crafting Your Writing

Once you have a first draft of your poem, you're ready to start shaping or crafting your writing. Read through the following hints and tips for perfecting your poem. If you use a different color pen to craft your poem, you'll see the changes happening very clearly.

TIP!
Have you used any "extra words" that aren't doing anything? Extra words are words like really, nice, and very. Can you get rid of them? Don't delete too many—your audience still has to understand!

TIP!
Is your title working as hard as it could? Is it too easy or too difficult? Is there a better title for what you've written? Experiment with different titles.

TIP!
Does your poem sound the way you want it to? Read it aloud to yourself first and then to a friend. Ask your audience for feedback. Would it be a good idea to add more sound effects?

TIP!
How does your poem look on the page? Are you happy with its structure? What happens if you change it from, for example, free verse into a sonnet? Is the meaning lost or improved?

TIP!
Use a thesaurus to help you choose even more precise describing words. This will help you pinpoint your details.

TIP!
If you haven't included a metaphor or a simile, can you add one? What effects does the metaphor or simile have on your poem?

TIP!
Ask friends to listen to your poem. What do they think the theme is? What suggestions do they have for improving your poem?

TIP!
Do you think your reader will feel the emotions you want? Can you shape your word choices to make them more extreme or more emotive?

TIP!
It's a good idea to leave your poem for a while and go do something else. Reflection time is a really important part of writing a poem. Go for a walk and come back to it later, or even in a few days. You'll be fresh and more perceptive about your work.

TIP!
If you aren't happy with your poem, you can always try again. It's not supposed to be a quick fix!

Think About This
Crafting Your Poetry

All poets edit and shape their work. Nobody writes exactly what they want to the first time. Poetry is about honing your word choices and polishing the language until it is as precise as possible. The Chilean Nobel Prize-winning poet Pablo Neruda always wrote in green ink because he thought that green was the color of hope. Maybe green ink will inspire you too!

Bibliography

The following works provided important sources of information for this book:

Carpenter, Humphrey, and Mari Prichard (eds.) *Oxford Companion to Children's Literature*. Oxford: Oxford University Press, 1995.

Davidson, George (ed.) *Roget's Thesaurus of English Words and Phrases*. London: Penguin Reference, 1994.

Drabble, Margaret (ed.) *Oxford Companion to English Literature*. Oxford: Oxford University Press, 2006.

Farrow, Rob, and Jennifer Curry (eds.) *I Remember, I Remember: Favourite Poems from Childhood*. London: Red Fox, 1993.

Gardner, Helen (ed.) *The New Oxford Book of Verse*. Oxford: Oxford University Press, 1989.

Hamilton, Ian (ed.) *The Oxford Companion to English Poetry*. Oxford: Oxford University Press, 1994.

More Poetry Please. London: Pheonix, 1993.

The New Oxford Dictionary of English. Oxford: Oxford University Press, 1998.

The Poems of Wilfred Owen. Ware: Wordsworth Editions Ltd, 1994

Somogyi, Nick de (ed.) *The Little Book of War Poems*. Malibu: Siena Publishing, 1999.

Wynne-Davies, Marion (ed.) *Prentice Hall Guide to English Literature*. London: Prentice Hall, 1990.

Glossary

abstract something that exists only as a thought or an idea rather than in a tangible form

alliteration repetition of the same sounds at the beginning of words within a sentence, phrase, or line of poetry

allusion reference to a person, place, or event from literature or history

anonymous unnamed

autobiographical about the author

cautionary tale story for children that teaches them about danger

cliché overused expression

cohere hold together

connotation set of ideas associated with a particular word

context setting or surrounding conditions that give meaning to the text

contrasting comparing two different things by putting them close to each other to emphasize their differences

end rhyme when only the last words in the lines rhyme

enjambment break in the middle of a sentence when one line of poetry runs on to the next

feint pretend to do one thing, then do something different

free verse form of poetry that does not have distinct patterns, and is written in the style of natural speech

guile cunning or deceit

imagery pictures created in your mind as you are reading

inference suggestion rather than an overt statement about something

internal rhyme when a word in the middle of a line rhymes with other words in a poem

ironic something that is the opposite of its usual or expected meaning

juxtaposition contrasting things placed side by side for purposes of comparison

labyrinth maze

lay up basketball shot made close to the net

metaphor literary device that draws a comparison between two seemingly unrelated things

metaphysical something spiritual that is beyond physical boundaries

meter arrangement of words in a line of poetry that gives it a particular rhythm

motif main image or theme in a poem

motivation the reason that a person does something

mythology traditional stories of a people, often concerning heroes and supernatural events

narrator speaker or "voice" in a poem

nostalgic longing for times past

onomatopoeia words that sound like the noise they make

pathos pity or sadness

personification when human characteristics or behavior are applied to nonhuman things

perspective point of view

pronoun word that substitutes for a noun, such as "I," "my," "his," or "her"

Pulitzer Prize annual American award for excellence in journalism, literature, or music

rhyme scheme fixed pattern of rhyming words in a poem

rhyming couplet two lines that have the same end rhyme; rhyming couplets are used at the end of sonnets

rite of passage significant event in a person's life

satirist writer who pokes fun at society and high-profile people

semantic field group of words about the same topic

simile figure of speech that compares two things using words such as "like," "as," "if," or "than"

sonnet form of verse with 14 lines and a consistent pattern of rhyme, ending in a rhyming couplet

sprung rhythm rhythm that changes throughout a poem, like the rhythm of natural speech

staccato short and sharp

stanza group of related lines in a poem that may have a particular pattern

stressed emphasized (the opposite is "unstressed")

structure form or shape of a poem; for example, the length of the lines, and whether the poem is split into stanzas and, if so, how long they are

tempo speed at which something moves along

theme key idea that the poet wants the reader to think about

verse line of poetry or, sometimes, poetry in general

wiles cunning plans, trickery

Find Out More

Books

Elizabeth, Mary. *Painless Poetry*. New York: Barron's Educational
  Services, 2011
  This is a good introduction to reading, analyzing, and writing
  poetry. It will help you overcome your fear of poetry through fun
  activities, brainteasers, and tips for making poetry fun.

Fehler, Gene. *Change-up: Baseball Poems*. New York: Clarion Books, 2009
  Enjoy this collection of poems about baseball.

Janeczko, Paul. *Seeing the Blue Between: Advice and Inspiration for Young
  Poets*. Somerville, Mass.: Candlewick Press, 2006
  Read this wealth of advice to young writers from 32 experienced
  poets. It contains letters and poems from these best-loved poets
  from around the world.

Johnson, Dave (ed.) *Movin': Teen Poets Take Voice*. New York: Orchard
  Books, 2000
  This is an anthology of poetry by kids from 5th grade on up, written
  for workshops at the New York Public Library. The poems cover
  real-life issues and topics that affect teens.

Llanas, Sheila Griffin (ed.) *Contemporary American Poetry: Not the End, But
  the Beginning*. Berkeley Height, N.J.: Enslow Publishers, 2010
  This is a collection of poetry featuring the work of poets from Billy
  Collins to Sylvia Plath.

Low, Alice. *The Fastest Game on Two Feet. And Other Poems about How Sports
  Began*. New York: Holiday House, 2009
  Read this compilation of poems by Alice Low about the origins of all
  different sports.

Roza, Greg. *Patterns in Poetry*. New York: Rosen Publishing, 2005
  Here is a useful guide to recognizing poetic form and meter.

Websites

www.gailmazur.com/listen.html
Listen to Gail Mazur discuss her poetry.

www.loc.gov/poetry/180
The American poet Billy Collins created the online poetry resource Poetry 180 for high schools in America. On the website, there is a poem for each day of the school year.

www.poetryarchive.org/poetryarchive/home.do
The Poetry Archive is continually building a huge online library of poetry selected by a panel of writers and critics. Poems can be searched by poet name, title, theme, and form.

www.poetryfoundation.org
The Poetry Foundation is dedicated to stimulating interest in poetry and keeping it alive in modern culture. The website contains extensive biographies of important poets, along with examples of their work.

http://poetryoutloud.org
Poetry Out Loud is a recitation competition funded by the National Endowment for the Arts and the Poetry Foundation.

http://writing.upenn.edu/pennsound/x/Komunyakaa.php
You can listen to Yusef Komunyakaa read his poem "Slam, Dunk, & Hook" here.

Acknowledgments
We would like to thank the following for permission to reproduce photographs: Dreamstime pp. 3 (Anthony Baggett), 7 (Olga Bogatyrenko), 20 (Kelpfish), 22 (1000words), 30 (Wimstime), 31 (Devy), 33 (Clearviewstock), 34 (Anthony Baggett), 39 (Iurii Osadchi), 52 (Glanum), 55 (Lightpoet); Corbis pp. 10 (Gib Martinez), 18 (Bettmann), 41 (Colin McPherson); Getty Images pp. 16, 23; Adam Horovitz p. 11; Library of Congress p. 32; Shutterstock pp. 4 (Pete Saloutos), 6 (Africa Studio), 8–9 (Warren Goldswain), 12–13 (Raphael Daniaud), 15 (Vasily Smirnov), 19 (Real Deal Photo), 21 (Boris Djuranovic), 25 (pio3), 27 (Dudarev Mikhail), 28–29 (Owen Fraser-Green), 36 (ollyy), 38 (MC_Noppadol), 40 (fstockfoto), 43 (muzsy), 44 (Oscar White), 45 (Richard Paul Kane), 46 (Eric Broder Van Dyke), 48 (Eric Broder Van Dyke), p. 50 (maxik); SuperStock p. 47 (Image Asset Management Ltd.); University of Chicago Press p. 29.

Index